Samuel French Acting Edition

Nourish the Beast

A Play in Two Acts

by Steve Tesich

SAMUELFRENCH.COM   SAMUELFRENCH.CO.UK

Copyright © 1974 by Steve Tesich
All Rights Reserved

NOURISH THE BEAST is fully protected under the copyright laws of the United States of America, the British Commonwealth, including Canada, and all other countries of the Copyright Union. All rights, including professional and amateur stage productions, recitation, lecturing, public reading, motion picture, radio broadcasting, television and the rights of translation into foreign languages are strictly reserved.

ISBN 978-0-573-61317-3

www.SamuelFrench.com
www.SamuelFrench.co.uk

For Production Enquiries

United States and Canada
Info@SamuelFrench.com
1-866-598-8449

United Kingdom and Europe
Plays@SamuelFrench.co.uk
020-7255-4302

Each title is subject to availability from Samuel French, depending upon country of performance. Please be aware that *NOURISH THE BEAST* may not be licensed by Samuel French in your territory. Professional and amateur producers should contact the nearest Samuel French office or licensing partner to verify availability.

CAUTION: Professional and amateur producers are hereby warned that *NOURISH THE BEAST* is subject to a licensing fee. Publication of this play(s) does not imply availability for performance. Both amateurs and professionals considering a production are strongly advised to apply to Samuel French before starting rehearsals, advertising, or booking a theatre. A licensing fee must be paid whether the title(s) is presented for charity or gain and whether or not admission is charged. Professional/Stock licensing fees are quoted upon application to Samuel French.

No one shall make any changes in this title(s) for the purpose of production. No part of this book may be reproduced, stored in a retrieval system, or transmitted in any form, by any means, now known or yet to be invented, including mechanical, electronic, photocopying, recording, videotaping, or otherwise, without the prior written permission of the publisher. No one shall upload this title(s), or part of this title(s), to any social media websites.

For all enquiries regarding motion picture, television, and other media rights, please contact Samuel French.

Please refer to page 67 for further copyright information.

NOURISH THE BEAST was first presented at The American Place Theatre, New York City, on May 9, 1973 under the title of "BABA GOYA." It was directed by Edwin Sherin; scenery by Karl Eigsti; lighting by Roger Morgan and costumes by Whitney Blausen. Compiled by Gigi Cascio. The associate director was Julia Miles. It appeared with the following cast in order of appearance:

CAST

GOYA	*Olympia Dukakis*
MARIO	*John Randolph*
OLD MAN	*Lou Gilbert*
BRUNO	*R. A. Dow*
SYLVIA	*Peggy Whitton*
ADOLF	*Ken Tigar*
CRIMINAL	*Randy Kim*
STUDLY	*David A. Butler*
CLIENT	*James Greene*

THE SETTING

All of the action takes place in a large room of an older home. Entrance from the street is through a door on stage left. Next to the door is a window overlooking the street. The window is elevated so that when one looks at the street one looks *down* into the street. On stage right there are two doors. One leads to a bathroom—the other to the room belonging to the old man. The doors are close together with nothing to distinguish one from the other. Stage center we find a large dining room table with three chairs. All three should not match. A little away from the table is an easy chair facing the audience and a sofa facing away from the audience. They also don't match. A kitchen area is in the background. Refrigerator and a stove should suffice. A prominently displayed radiator. A stairway leads to the three rooms upstairs. It's not necessary to have the doors to the rooms seen, but the corridor leading to them should be visible. Other items such as lamps or any other pieces of furniture as deemed fit. The set should look realistic but not cluttered.

Nourish the Beast

ACT ONE

SCENE 1

It's morning. [Sound cue 1.] GOYA comes down, makes coffee. MARIO'S coming down the stairway. By the looks of him he's just gotten out of bed. He scratches himself . . . rubs his eyes . . . then when he stops at the foot of the stairway he opens his mouth to yawn but instead of a yawn we hear a dog howl. [Sound cue 2.] MARIO grabs his throat. He seems stunned. The dog howls again. [Sound cue 3.] MARIO runs over to the window. Looks out. Rubs one eye. Cleans the window. Looks out again. [Sound cue 4.]

MARIO. Can't be. (*Runs to the chest of drawers. Pulls out a telescope. Runs back to the window.*) Can't be that big. (*Looks through telescope.*) It's bigger. Amazing. Must be a world's record. (*Looks intently through the telescope.*) Must be a hormone imbalance. (GOYA *sees* MARIO *staring through the window. She wonders what he's looking at. She'd like to know but it's not her way to ask.* MARIO'S *like a statue.*) Amazing. (GOYA'S *pondering. Should she ask or shouldn't she. She opens her mouth to say something and the dog howls once again.* [Sounds cue 5.])

GOYA. All right. I give up. What's going on? (*Without taking his telescope off the window* MARIO *waves to her to come over.*)

MARIO. If you want to see something amazing . . . (GOYA *walks toward him slowly. She doesn't like to be called. She walks toward him as if somebody's pushing her. She lights a cigarette on the way as if making sure her lack of haste is understood.*)

GOYA. Well . . .

MARIO. Look. (*She looks through the window.*)

GOYA. Good God.

MARIO. Isn't it amazing. (GOYA *takes his telescope. Looks through it.*) . . . I'd say it's the horniest looking dog I've ever seen. [*Sound cue 6.*])

GOYA. . . . look at it . . . You'd think he'd got five legs.

MARIO. It's a whopper all right. Reminds me of a friend of mine from high school. His name, appropriately enough, was Lenny Long, and ole Lenny had this trick he'd do for us in the locker room . . . He would sit down . . . put a cigarette on his kneecap and knock it off with his you know what. (*He demonstrates with his clenched fist.* GOYA *looks at him.*)

GOYA. Well, now that we've had our morning prayers let's move on to something else. I've got a lot of work to do.

MARIO. In retrospect I wonder if perhaps Lenny didn't have a touch of homosexual in him.

GOYA. Lenny! How about the rest of you guys . . . sitting there watching this character flick cigarettes off his knees with his . . . (*She stops. Dog howls again.* [*Sounds cue 7.*] SYLVIA's *voice is heard from upstairs.*)

SYLVIA. Hush, Dodo, you hear me . . . hush. (GOYA *and* MARIO *look at each other and then look upstairs and then at each other again.*)

GOYA. I should've known. It's Sylvia's dog.

MARIO. Funny name for a horny dog . . . Dodo.

GOYA. Last time she came home she brought that kitten with her.

MARIO. Betcha anything this Dodo ate the kitten.

GOYA. The time before that it was a guinea pig.

MARIO. Grandma ate the pig.

GOYA. What are you talking about?

ACT I NOURISH THE BEAST 7

MARIO. Sylvia's guinea pig. Remember . . . I took it to that little Sicilian lady . . . poor thing, I thought, all alone and everything . . . maybe a pet would cheer her up . . . Well . . . I guess they don't keep pets in the old country . . . Grandma took good care of it for one winter and then she ate it. Said it tasted like rabbit.

GOYA. That cute little guinea pig? You sure she's Sicilian?

MARIO. That's what she said.

GOYA. She's probably German. One of them carnivorous Germans. (*She looks out of the window.* [*Sound cue 8.*]) Maybe she'd like a dog. (*She goes to the kitchen area. Comes back carrying a Turkish coffee pot and two demitasse cups. She places the coffee and the cup on the table. Sits down. A loud noise is heard from upstairs. The noise is a mixture between a sigh and a groan. It belongs to* SYLVIA. GOYA's *not moved by it.*) I wonder how long she plans to keep that up.

MARIO. It sounds like she's just warming up, to me. I used to be a janitor in an opera house . . . and that's how they did it . . . They'd be there . . . sitting down tying their shoelaces and screaming at the top of their lungs.

GOYA. Your coffee's ready. (*He comes over and sits down.*) Did she say anything to you?

MARIO. Not really . . . I just got back from work last night and there she was standing outside the door. Sylvia, I said. Mario, she says, and starts crying. At first I thought she was crying because she was glad to see me . . . but then she kept it up. Couldn't be that glad, I figured. And then I thought, maybe she found out about my condition . . . you know . . . crying because I was going to die and all . . . but she kept it up. Couldn't be that sorry to see me go, I figured. So I finally asked her. Why are you crying. If you only knew, she says, and erupts with such a barrage of snots and tears that I didn't know whether to offer her sympathy or an antihistamine.

GOYA. She cried all night . . . poor little phony. You think she'd be exhausted.

MARIO. According to an article in *Today's Health* people who cry at night aren't nearly as sick as what they call mid-day weepers.

GOYA. Taking all that into consideration, Mario, I think we better get our rear in gear and start solving some of these problems. I've let things slide . . . I feel it . . . things are slipping through my fingers . . . People are running around the house doing all kinds of weird things without so much as a word of explanation . . . You too. Fine time you picked to die.

MARIO. I didn't really choose when . . .

GOYA. We'll get to that later. Now . . . the way I see it, these are the major areas of concern . . .

MARIO. Hold it. (*He takes out a used envelope and a pencil from his pocket.*) Shoot, as Bruno would say.

GOYA. First of all we have to find out why Sylvia came home . . . get to the bottom of her chronic "secret sorrow" and then get her out of here.

MARIO. But she's your own daughter, Goya.

GOYA. I can't let family ties interfere with my family affairs. (MARIO *writes.*) Next comes Bruno . . . he's been awfully depressed. It takes him half an hour to come down the stairs . . . he gulps his coffee . . . eats fruit cocktail out of a can . . . he took a shower with his socks on the other day.

MARIO. (*Writes.*) I got it.

GOYA. Then there's the old man. He was a nice old man for a while and now, to be blunt, he's rapidly turning into a mean old man. I know . . . I'm partially to blame because I let him linger on under the false assumption that someday . . . well . . . you know . . .

MARIO. (*With relish writes.*) Yes, I got it.

GOYA. (*Waits for him to finish.*) I think that about does it.

MARIO. What about cheese?

GOYA. What cheese?

MARIO. We're all out of cheese . . . and Sylvia likes cheese.

GOYA. All right, put down cheese. Let's hear what you've got. (MARIO *sits up straighter. Coughs. Smooths out the envelope.*)

MARIO. Let's see. Things to be done. Soothe Sylvia, brighten Bruno and meliorate the mean old man.

GOYA. Oh, common . . .

MARIO. It's more concise this way. And then there's cheese. (*Outside the house Dodo, the dog, lets out a howl.* [*Sound cue 9.*]) What about Dodo?

GOYA. The hell with Dodo.

MARIO. Knowing Sylvia she probably didn't feed the poor thing.

GOYA. All right . . . get him some food. (MARIO *writes.*) What did you put down?

MARIO. Just what you said . . . dogfood.

GOYA. Let me see. (*Takes envelope.*) Nourish the beast! Is that what I said?

MARIO. It's got a nice ring to it. Considering my condition . . . I just might drop dead in the street . . . and it pleases me to think that when they go through my pockets they stumble on this mysterious notation: Nourish the beast.

GOYA. Look here, Mario . . . if you feel the Maker calling you to his bosom then I guess you have to answer the call . . . All I got to say is . . . you picked a helluva time to croak.

MARIO. Who picked the time . . . what . . . I was born and before I knew what was happening I started living . . . I didn't like the way I was living . . . so I started waiting around for things to get better . . . Things, I figured had to get better. Things got worse. Well, I figured, at least they can't get any worse. They got worse. And then they got even worse than that. I was born into a dirty and rotten world and progress being what it is it got dirtier and more rotten. Since yesterday its got dirtier. In the last half hour . . . (*Looks out of window.*) It wasn't that dirty when I got out of bed . . . now look at it . . . can't find one ripe tomato in the whole city . . . apples are all mealy . . . cucumbers are bitter . . . lettuce is wilted . . . I never have exact change for a bus . . . when I do I can't find a seat . . . the mops they give me at work leave those little strings all over the place . . . they closed down another cafeteria . . . I never run into old friends the way I used to . . . nobody plays dominoes anymore . . . they left me out of the phone book again . . . I have no idea what Eric Severeid is talking about . . .

GOYA. HOLD IT! ENOUGH! DIE IF YOU MUST! (*Silence.*)

MARIO. I just wanted to make sure you understood.

GOYA. I understand. Only . . . I hope you understand . . . that if something does happen to you . . .

MARIO. You mean like death.

GOYA. Yes . . . I hope you realize I'll be sadder than hell.

MARIO. That's understood.

GOYA. I also hope you realize that I can't go around beating my breasts over it . . . It's not in my nature.

MARIO. Believe me, Goya, when I say that breasts like yours were not meant to be beaten.

GOYA. No poetry, please. If you die I'm going to have to get another husband . . . and I'll probably get him the same way I got you . . . I just can't wait around until somebody nice comes along.

MARIO. I already took care of that. I put an ad in the paper myself.

GOYA. You didn't.

MARIO. It should be in this morning's edition.

GOYA. You little sweetheart.

MARIO. No poetry, please.

GOYA. In that case we're all set to kick off the fall schedule. First item on the schedule is Sylvia . . . SYLVIA! COMMON DOWN HERE!

MARIO. Don't you think a subtle approach would work better on her?

GOYA. Fine. I'll be subtle. First I got to get her down here. SYLVIA . . . COMMON DOWN, DEAR . . . If you want some understanding you better get to me before noon . . . SYLVIA!

MARIO. That must be what Dr. Meriweather of the Institute for Family Relations calls the hand grenade approach.

GOYA. SYLVIA! We're waiting . . . (*The door to the* OLD MAN'S *room opens and the* OLD MAN *comes out with note paper. He looks terribly irritated. Both* GOYA *and* MARIO *see him and brace themselves for the inevitable tirade.*)

OLD MAN. What the hell . . . what the goddamned hell *is* all this . . . First I hear howling . . . then I hear some madman screaming about a world's record . . . then I hear HUSH DODO . . . then I hear somebody crying . . . then I start hearing SYLVIA! SYLVIA! I wait . . . and by God it comes again . . . SYLVIA! SYLVIA! Why don't you just come in my room and drop a cannonball down my ears. I'll go deaf if this keeps up, I'm warning you. I'll just sit down and go deaf and then you'll be sorry. You'll come home and ask me if there were any phone calls for you . . . You might feel like talking to me . . . You might even want to know what time it is because your watch stopped . . . and I won't be able to tell you a thing because I won't know what the hell you're talking about because you drove me deaf. Now do you understand!

GOYA. Yes, grandpa. (*This word hits the* OLD MAN *like a slap on the face.*)

OLD MAN. Grampa! (*Takes a threatening step toward* GOYA.) How many times do I have to tell you . . . Do I have to get a lawyer for Chrissakes . . . I'm not . . . never was . . . and never will be yours or anybody else's grampa. Is that clear? I see it's not. Alright. I'll fix you. I'll blast you. You'll see. I'll blast you right out of here.

(*He spins around dramatically and stomps away in a blind rage . . . so blind in fact that he goes into the bathroom instead of his room . . . slamming the door shut after him.* GOYA's *not looking.* MARIO *is. She looks at* MARIO *as if to ask: Did he stomp into the bathroom again . . .* MARIO *nods . . . Yes he did. They continue to brace themselves. The bathroom door flies open and the* OLD MAN *stomps out.* MARIO *and* GOYA *are looking away from him.*) Don't think I made a mistake. I went in there on purpose . . . there was no mistake. I want that understood. I had business in there. (*And to prove that he had business in there he goes through the motions of zipping his fly with such dramatic intensity that he practically rips it off. Then he stomps away into his room and slams the door shut.*)

GOYA. Got to meliorate that mean old man. (MARIO *looks at his notes.*)

MARIO. I got it down. (BRUNO *appears at the top of the stairway and begins lumbering his way down.* GOYA, *to make sure* MARIO *notices, does an imitation of* BRUNO's *walk . . . arms hanging on her side . . . head bowed . . . exactly the way* BRUNO *is.* MARIO *looks at her . . . looks at* BRUNO . . . BRUNO *finally arrives at the foot of the stairway. He's dressed in a police uniform. Takes the gun from the drawer and looks at it.*)

GOYA. Before you shoot yourself I'd like a word with you. (BRUNO *puts gun in holster. Looks at* GOYA *who shouts.*) Why don't you brighten up, Bruno?

MARIO. You're getting more subtle by the minute.

GOYA. Come here, son. How about some coffee.

BRUNO. All right. (GOYA *pours out some coffee into* MARIO's *demitasse cup.* BRUNO *comes over and without sitting down he chugs the coffee in one gulp.*)

GOYA. Care for another shot.

BRUNO. All right. (GOYA *pours out another cup.* BRUNO *chugs it in one gulp.*)

GOYA. Bruno, my son, that's Turkish coffee you're annihilating. It costs two fifty a pound. I get it for two ten because I tell this old Turk I hate Greeks. If I can perjure myself the least you can do is enjoy it.

BRUNO. I enjoy it.

GOYA. Don't tell me that . . . You don't drink Turkish coffee standing up . . . It's sit down coffee . . . Bend your legs, Bruno . . . You look like you're standing inside a holster. Sit down. (*He sits.*) There . . . doesn't that feel better?

BRUNO. No.

GOYA. (*Leaning over him.*) Bruno . . . I'm not one of those commissions investigating police corruption . . . don't be so defensive . . . This is your little ole mother you're talking to. (MARIO *lets out a chortle.*) Did you want to laugh about something, Mario?

MARIO. Yes I did. But I changed my mind.

GOYA. Could you change it a little more quietly? I'm talking to my son, the Fifth Amendment, here. Now where was I?

BRUNO. You were being a little ole mother. (*He and* MARIO *exchange a conspiratory glance.*)

GOYA. What's this . . . you didn't tell me you were taking a stenography course on the sly. Are you listening to this, Mario?

MARIO. Yes, don't you want me to?

GOYA. Of course I do. I need a witness with his kind. Bruno . . . look at me when I talk to you. (*He looks at her.*) Don't look at me like that, Bruno. I'm not a dentist. You know Mario's been very worried about you. (MARIO *protests with his hands.* GOYA *ignores him.*) He's got enough to worry about, the poor thing. Look at him, Bruno. (BRUNO *looks at* MARIO *and* MARIO's *on the spot. Has to pretend he's worried.*) He's talking about dying.

BRUNO. I know. I don't want him to die.

GOYA. Well, you're killing him.

MARIO. Let's hold it right there. I wouldn't blame Bruno for . . .

GOYA. Just because you have one foot in the grave is

no reason to put the other in your mouth, Mario. Now why don't you go and get me the paper.

BRUNO. I'll get it.

GOYA. I like the way Mario gets it better. Adios, Mario. (MARIO *leaves.* GOYA *light a cigarette.*) Care for a cigarette?

BRUNO. That's how we treat criminals down at the station. First we offer them a cigarette and then if they refuse we beat them up. I wonder how many people started smoking in police stations.

GOYA. So now your mother is a police station.

BRUNO. No, but we did have a guy down there who was a marvel at getting confessions. He'd hug the suspects and break into tears . . . he'd tell them how he's going to get fired if he doesn't get a conviction soon . . . how his kids are starving . . . his wife dying of scurvy or something . . . he got more confessions that way. We called him Mother Sarge.

GOYA. How has the word mother come to mean so many unpleasant things?

BRUNO. I think mothers had something to do with it.

GOYA. All any mother wants is for her kids to be happy.

BRUNO. Speaking for the kids . . . all they want is for the mothers to be happy.

GOYA. Mothers can't be happy if their kids aren't happy.

BRUNO. Mothers should try.

GOYA. I'm not going to beg you, Bruno, and I refuse to resort to threats . . . It's not in my nature. Let's just say . . . you're killing your father and you're well on your way to killing me. If that's what you want . . . If that'll make you happy . . . Then you might as well pull out . . .

BRUNO. All right, ma . . . all right . . . don't tell me to pull out my gun and shoot you again. I'll speak. It's the orphanage business . . . it's crept into my mind again.

GOYA. Well tell it to creep out again. You're not an

orphan anymore. Do I treat you like an orphan? Haven't I been a real mother to you?

BRUNO. You're the most real mother I've ever seen. Believe me . . . when conversation turns to real mothers I always bring up your name. But I can't get that orphanage business out of my head. It keeps coming back . . . and somehow it's affecting my job now . . . I'm tired of dragging criminals down to the station. I know for example, that I'll catch some orphaney looking criminal today . . . I know it . . . and already I'm sweating it . . . what am I going to do with him?

GOYA. Bring him home for coffee if that'll make you happy.

BRUNO. And then there's Sylvia.

GOYA. I knew there was more to it.

BRUNO. I could tell she was coming home again.

GOYA. Did you two get in a fight already?

BRUNO. No. She came home last night and pretended to be crying. I pretended to be asleep but she pretended not to notice and kept right on crying. She's so goddamned phony.

GOYA. I know. But this is her home and if she wants to come home I can't chase her out right away.

BRUNO. But why does she have to have such phony excuses for coming home? After every election she shows up and starts snotting about the state of the union.

GOYA. That's what phonies cry about.

BRUNO. And another thing . . . how come she doesn't know that I'm an orphan? I mean . . . she thinks I'm her brother and I just don't feel like being a brother to a phony sister like that.

GOYA. I tried to tell her once. I said, you know Bruno's not your real brother. And she said, you can say that again.

BRUNO. Well . . . I'm going to tell her.

GOYA. Go ahead, and if she gives you any lip about being an orphan you can always come back and call her a bastard.

BRUNO. I didn't know that.

GOYA. Well, now you do. But use it sparingly. I never married her father and for all I know nobody else did either.

BRUNO. How come?

GOYA. Because he was such a phony. You don't think she gets it from me do you? Now cheer up son, so mother can move on to other things. (BRUNO *gets up, looks at his watch. Goes toward the door.* GOYA *hugs him.* [*Sound cue 10.*] *He looks over her shoulder, through the window.*)

BRUNO. God, would you look at that dog.

GOYA. I already did.

BRUNO. Did Mario ever tell you about this guy he knew . . . Lenny Long.

GOYA. (*Throws cigarette on the floor. Crushes it.*) I believe he did. (*As* BRUNO *is going out,* MARIO *comes in carrying a newspaper.*)

BRUNO. See you this evening.

MARIO. I hope so. (BRUNO *goes out.* MARIO *shuts the door.*) I see you fixed him up.

GOYA. One down . . . Is it in the paper? I don't want to seem greedy . . . I'm just curious . . . (MARIO *leafs through the back portion of the paper.*)

MARIO. Here it is. WANTED: potential husband to assume full duties and responsibilities of the same. Must have a steady job and not hang around the house all day. Apply in person and ask for Goya. And the address.

GOYA. It's a very nice ad . . . and I certainly have no right to complain . . . but you should've put something in there about me not wanting a German . . . I betcha anything Adolf shows up again.

MARIO. Germans are human too.

GOYA. Some Germans . . . some I haven't met . . . and I've met all of them. Oh, Mario, I don't want you to die.

MARIO. Don't worry . . . somebody nice'll come along.

GOYA. That's just it . . . what if some real stud answers the ad . . . and I really get the hots for him . . . and you're still alive.

MARIO. I think that should be enough to do me in.

GOYA. (*Rises.*) Give me a kiss.

MARIO. Why not. (*They kiss.* GOYA *feels his back pocket.*)

GOYA. What else did you buy?

MARIO. Nothing.

GOYA. Get off it, Mario.

MARIO. You said buy a paper and I bought a paper.

GOYA. And what else?

MARIO. Nothing else.

GOYA. What stupid magazine did you throw away your money on this time?

MARIO. I told you . . . (MARIO *gives in. Pulls out a magazine.* GOYA *reads.*)

GOYA. *Psychology Today* . . . oh, Mario.

MARIO. It's got an interesting article in there. "Why People Lie."

GOYA. Yes, Mario, why do they?

MARIO. I don't know, I haven't read it yet . . . (*A long drawn out wail of a cry is heard from* SYLVIA *upstairs.*)

GOYA. There she goes again . . . God forgive me but I just can't face her now . . . any good movies around? (*Looks through paper.*) No. But I'll go anyway. You going to work?

MARIO. Might as well.

GOYA. I'll walk to the subway with you. I hate to say this, about anybody who's even part female . . . but what she needs is a good screw . . . and once she finds out Bruno's not her brother . . . (*They start walking out.*)

MARIO. Part of the problem in today's society is that people can no longer differentiate good screws from bad screws. At least that's what Paul Harvey seems to think. (*They walk out. Almost simultaneously* SYLVIA *appears at the top of the stairway. Her pose in descending down the stairway is such that her face is hidden in one hand . . . the other hand being used for support. She seems to be assuming that* GOYA'S *still in the house.*)

SYLVIA. Oh, mother . . . mother . . . mother . . . mother . . . your little sinner is back . . . your naughty little Sylvia has done it this time . . . No . . . please don't ask me what it is . . . It's horrible . . . It's ghastly . . . if you only knew . . . (*She stops at the foot of the stairway . . . puts her head on the bannister and lets out a cry. The* OLD MAN *leaps out of his room.*)

OLD MAN. Shut up already.

SYLVIA. Oh . . . I thought . . . where's mother?

OLD MAN. She went to a movie, you little phony.

SYLVIA. What a mean old man you are. If I wasn't so heartbroken I'd tell you to go to hell.

OLD MAN. So you need a good screw, do you!

SYLVIA. Even if I did . . . (*Looks him over.*) Chances seem slim of getting one here. Are you one of those things Mother took in?

OLD MAN. I am what I am . . . which is more than I can say for you. I heard everything. I'm not deaf yet you know . . . You and that Dodo of yours.

SYLVIA. Poor Dodo . . . animals are so intuitive . . . he senses my grief . . . my burning sense of guilt . . .

OLD MAN. I hear he's got a real whopper.

SYLVIA. You're probably suffering from inflation . . . People on fixed incomes . . . pensions . . . social security and the like are the ones who suffer the most . . . and I've added to their suffering . . . yours too . . . is that why you hate me . . . You sense the wrong I've done . . . Does it show? . . . I feel that it shows.

OLD MAN. I once ate a Hostess Twinkie and got sick to my stomach. I vomited in the street and everybody thought I was drunk . . . but I wasn't . . . it was that Twinkie that did me in . . . and that's what *you* remind me of . . . a Hostess Twinkie.

SYLVIA. Well, you're no cupcake yourself, handsome. But go ahead . . . hate me . . . I've brought it upon myself . . . It must be hard for you . . . fixed income and all . . . I'm sorry . . . Forgive me, Grampa. (*The* OLD MAN *reacts to the word "grampa" the way he did before.*)

OLD MAN. Grampa! Somebody's spreading rumors again. Well, if that's how they want to fight. All right. I'll blast you. You'll see. (*Starts shaking from frustration . . . spins around and stomps away right into the bathroom. Stomps out almost immediately zipping up his fly with dramatic intensity and stomps away into his room.*)

SYLVIA. That was quick. ([*Sound cue 11.*] *She sits down at the table. Sighs. Drops her head on the newspaper. Belches. Looks around. Drops her head again in a posture of total despair.*)

(*BLACKOUT.*)

ACT ONE

SCENE 2

Same as in Scene 1. It's a few hours later. SYLVIA *hasn't moved from her place and her posture at the table is the same as it was.* GOYA *is standing behind her.* SYLVIA *is crying and* GOYA *is comforting her with her hand . . . patting her head . . . but* GOYA's *face registers anything but sympathy. At times she even mouths the word "Phony" while her hand sympathizes on top of* SYLVIA's *head.*

GOYA. There . . . there . . . Mother's here. Mother understands.

SYLVIA. I came down here and nobody was here except this mean old creature . . . My own mother, whom I haven't seen in years couldn't even wait to comfort me.

GOYA. Well, I waited for a few years for you to come home and then I went to a movie. Some movie. I think they had a special . . . anyone who came in with smelly underwear got in free . . . and let me tell you, dear, there wasn't a paying customer in the whole place. I had a flasher on my left and a drunk on my right. So I move and sit down next to this character who's playing with himself through a popcorn box . . . I want to call the usher and I look again and he is the usher.

SYLVIA. Men are so horrible, aren't they, mother? (GOYA *looks at* SYLVIA.)

GOYA. I wouldn't give you a dime for some women I know either.

SYLVIA. I got a divorce, you know.

GOYA. I didn't know you were married.

SYLVIA. I was.

GOYA. Well, congratulations. I hope you were very happy.

SYLVIA. Happy! You have to be an idiot to be a married woman.

GOYA. I wouldn't give you a dime for some divorcees I know either.

SYLVIA. All he did was wash his car and lie about the miles per gallon he was getting. I married him because he was a liberal and you know what he did . . . He forced me to get pregnant just so I could get an abortion and test the legality of some law or other. So I had an abortion. Then I divorced him and proceeded to do some ghastly things which culminated in an absolute nightmare.

GOYA. You don't have to tell me if you don't want to.

SYLVIA. I slept with a black man, mother.

GOYA. It's better than staying up all night, dear.

SYLVIA. I was in a pornographic movie.

GOYA. I just came back from one.
SYLVIA. I took drugs; I sold drugs. I rolled drunks . . . I was a shoplifter.
GOYA. Prices being what they are . . . who can blame you.
SYLVIA. I turned my back on morality and decency. I ridiculed honesty and laughed at the ideas of the struggling masses. I lived like an animal.
GOYA. At least you had a good time.
SYLVIA. And then . . . (*She starts sobbing.*)
GOYA. There . . . there . . .
SYLVIA. And then I . . . (*She's choked with sobs.* GOYA *mouths the word "phony" a couple of times.*)
GOYA. Mother's here . . . Mother understands.
SYLVIA. And then . . . in the national election . . . I voted for Nixon.
GOYA. You little bitch! (*Pushes* SYLVIA *to floor then moves chair close to table.* OLD MAN *flies out of his room in a rage with a belt in hand.*)
OLD MAN. NIXON! You little bitch you! And me with fixed income. Let me at her! (*He rushes at* SYLVIA. SYLVIA *rolls on ground* U. S. R. *of radiator.* GOYA *stops him.* SYLVIA *cries.*)
GOYA. I'll handle this.
OLD MAN. Let me at her. I'll blast her.
GOYA. Take it easy, grampa. (OLD MAN *freezes momentarily and then begins shaking.*)
OLD MAN. Grampa! You're no better than she . . . I'll have to blast both of you . . . I'll . . . I'll do it . . . (*He spins around and begins stomping away right toward the bathroom.*)
GOYA. NOT THAT WAY! (*The* OLD MAN *changes his course like a pin ball and stomps away into his room.* SYLVIA's *crying even louder. Dodo starts howling outside.* [*Sound cue 12.*]) Shut up, Sylvia. Hush, Dodo! Enough! (*Neither of them do.* GOYA *goes to the window. Opens it and throws magazines at Dodo. Dodo lets out*

a painful howl, [Sound cue 13.] and stops. SYLVIA *screams.* GOYA *picks up another load of magazines . . . throws it at* OLD MAN'S *door . . . he just escapes.*) Look, dear, let's not let politics come between us . . . Your rotten voting habits are your own affair.

SYLVIA. I did it to spite my husband . . . Now the whole country hates me . . . it's all my fault.

GOYA. Don't blame yourself, dear. There were other morons who voted the way you did.

SYLVIA. I hate myself.

GOYA. You shouldn't do that . . . That's what mothers are for. Look, honey, I wish I could take the time to make you feel better . . . but I've got other things on my mind . . . You know Mario's going to die.

SYLVIA. Oh, mother . . . poor mother . . . you're going to be all alone.

GOYA. Never can tell, dear.

SYLVIA. I'll stay with you. The two of us will live together. We're in the same boat, you and I.

GOYA. I don't think we're even in the same sea, dear. But thank you, anyway.

SYLVIA. We'll live together and grow old together. We'll have nothing to do with men. We'll wear dowdy clothes and plant flowers.

GOYA. It's nice of you to paint such a rosy future for me, but . . .

SYLVIA. We'll grieve our lives away like a couple of nuns. I must admit, mother, it did shock me a little the way you didn't grieve for any of your husbands. I mean those newspaper ads . . . no sooner did they die than you'd invite every Tom, Dick and Harry . . .

GOYA. Just for the record, dear . . . their names were Peter, Ferdinand and Marko . . . and Mario of course.

SYLVIA. In any case . . . thing'll be different from now on. You and I . . . (*Something attracts her attention in the newspaper. She looks hard at the paper, reads some of the ad out loud, and then begins screaming in total frustration.*) MOTHER! YOU DID IT AGAIN! (*Throws newspaper* U. S.)

GOYA. No I didn't . . . Mario did it. That crazy Mario . . . What'll he think of next? (SYLVIA *starts bawling, snotting at the nose and in general betraying quite a few signs of envy.*)

SYLVIA. You're horrible . . . I can't even have one decent husband and you're working your fifth.

GOYA. It's really no work, dear, once you get used to it. Don't worry, we'll find you a man.

SYLVIA. I think men are gross.

GOYA. Some are . . . some are downright puny.

SYLVIA. I think you're gross. You have no heart.

GOYA. I gave it away, dear.

SYLVIA. That's not all you gave away. Sex at your age . . . Aren't you ashamed?

GOYA. I am . . . but I've learned to live with it. What can I do, dear, my bed sags on one side . . . I need a man for balance so I don't fall out.

SYLVIA. Then get a new bed.

GOYA. I guess I'm sentimental. I like the old one. (*Seeing as how she's losing the battle rapidly* SYLVIA *resorts to tears again.*)

SYLVIA. Nobody loves me.

GOYA. There, there, dear (SYLVIA *starts towards her.*) . . . somebody must. (SYLVIA *stops.*)

SYLVIA. I don't even know why I bothered coming home. (*She runs up stairs.*)

GOYA. Don't worry . . . I'm sure you'll think of something. (SYLVIA *breaks into sobs and disappears into her upstairs rooms.*) A phony . . . My God . . . you'd think she went to college and got a degree in it. (*Doorbell rings.* GOYA *puts out cigarette and goes to the door.* ADOLF *remains in the doorway out of sight of the audience. She sees him, pushes door shut, then puts on safety chain.*)

ADOLF. Good evening. I'm looking for Goya.

GOYA. What can she do for you?

ADOLF. I happened to be leafing through the Post . . . usually I leaf through the New York Times . . . but it just so happened that I happened to be leafing through the Post . . .

GOYA. Would you mind leafing a little faster?

ADOLF. Why should I mind? You say faster . . . I go faster . . . you say slow . . . I go slow. Whatever you say I do.

GOYA. Why don't you take off your hat or whatever you call that thing? There . . . now why don't you take off your wig? Now what do you want, baldie?

ADOLF. As I was leafing through the Post I happened to be struck by an ad . . .

GOYA. You better go home before you get struck by something else. This is a bad neighborhood. Everybody on the block is out on bail.

ADOLF. It says here . . . potential husband to assume . . .

GOYA. Hold it. Don't assume nothing. First of all, I don't like your potential. Secondly, ADOLF, I told you when Peter died I wasn't interested . . . I told you when Ferdinand went that you can go too . . . and I never forgave you for not showing up after Marko's death.

ADOLF. You must have me confused with somebody else.

GOYA. What's there to confuse . . . you're German.

ADOLF. I've never seen you before and I told you the last time that I'm not German.

GOYA. And I told you the last time that you were.

ADOLF. I have changed.

GOYA. You look every bit as German as you ever did. Besides . . . what kind of a man are you . . . have you no pride . . . couldn't you've found a wife in all this time?

ADOLF. I did. I was married but my wife happened to die.

GOYA. Your wife dies and you start looking for another one right away. You're a cold hearted bunch . . . you Germans. What's that you got there?

ADOLF. I happen to have a bottle of booze in my possession. (GOYA *takes the bottle*.)

GOYA. I'll take it. I'm an alcoholic you know. Forget the ad, Adolf . . . it was all a mistake . . . My husband, as far as I know, is still alive.

ADOLF. Too bad. Maybe some other time.

GOYA. Sure thing . . . when the last man on earth dies and Dodo's not available . . . give me a buzz. In the meanwhile you might check out this Sicilian woman who gobbles up bunnies and guinea pigs . . . She's German too . . . Guten abend, mein Herrn.

ADOLF. Guten abend, Frau Goya. (GOYA *shuts the door. Spits.*)

GOYA. (*Leaning on door.*) Frau! Ugh. Frau. Leave it to Germans to take a nice word like woman and turn her into a Frau. Frau Goya. Sounds like a German Betty Crocker. Ugh! (*Opens the bottle. Takes a swig.*) It sure doesn't taste like tomato juice. (*Laughs.*) Got to hand it to Adolf. He always brings something to soothe the nasty impression he makes. (*Takes another swig.*) Poor man . . . he had hair when he first came. (*Takes another swig.*) Or maybe it was always a wig. (*Another swig.*) In any case . . . it was a better looking wig than the one he's got now. It's horrible . . . to feel guilty for turning down a German . . . I have nothing against Germans as such . . . there are Germans and then there are Germans. It's my misfortune that I only run into the latter . . . or is it the former . . . Oh, hell, they're all alike . . . (*[Sound cue 14.] She takes another swig. A police siren is heard outside. Gun shots.* DODO *starts barking.* GOYA *takes a swig and crosses to the door.*) Here we go again . . . What a neighborhood . . . Better lock up the door and get drunk. (GOYA *locks door, and goes to the kitchen.*) This is no time to be sober. (*Footsteps are heard outside the door, they come closer. A noise as if someone is fighting outside* GOYA's *door. Banging is heard on the door.*) I didn't do it, and I don't know who did! (GOYA *picks up glass and brings it to table.* BRUNO's *voice is heard outside the door.*)

BRUNO. Ma . . . it's me . . . Open up.
GOYA. Bruno . . . (*She opens the door.* BRUNO *bursts in carrying an* ORIENTAL YOUTH. *They are handcuffed,* ORIENTAL'S *got the camera.*)
BRUNO. Can't explain now . . . the cops are out there . . . if they come . . . tell them . . . I don't care . . . just get rid of them . . . (*Footsteps are heard outside the door . . .* BRUNO *looks for a place to go. Runs for the john. Drags the* ORIENTAL *with him inside the john and shuts the door. As soon as the bathroom door is shut knocking is heard . . . doorbell rings.* GOYA *heads for the door . . . takes a swig from the bottle on the way.* GOYA *primps, removes pencil from hair. Settles breasts in brassiere, then reaches behind to make shirt tighter. Opens the door and blocks the entrance with her body. Cop remains offstage.*)
GOYA. Good evening, Studly.
STUDLY. Hate to disturb you, m'am.
GOYA. Oh, that's all right. I'm already disturbed as you can see.
STUDLY. A man just had his camera ripped right off his shoulder . . . we thought we saw the suspect come in here.
GOYA. You've got good eyes . . . no . . . lovely eyes. The suspect did come in here . . . or tried . . . But I chased him away . . . A German fellow right . . . with a scroungy looking wig. Calls everybody and his uncle Frau . . . killed his wife I think . . . He went . . . hold on a second . . . I think I have his address. (*Goes to the chest of drawers and produces a card.*) He left his card last time he was here . . . there's his address. (*Gives card to cop.*) It's rough out there, eh?
STUDLY. Happens after every election.
GOYA. Well . . . drop by again . . . during primaries or something.
STUDLY. I just might do that.
GOYA. I just might be here. (*She shuts the door. Deep*

sigh.) God, how I love a pair of eyes like that . . . when they're perched on a body like that . . . ([*Sound cue 15.*] *She remembers about* BRUNO . . . *goes to the bathroom and opens the door. Somebody is heard taking a leak inside.* [*Sound cue 16.*] BRUNO's *head appears.*)

BRUNO. Mother, can't you see . . .

GOYA. I can . . . I can . . . and let me tell you Dodo's got nothing on him. (BRUNO *comes halfway out of the john . . . his other hand still attached to the criminal. The criminal is still taking a leak.* BRUNO *points gun,* GOYA *peeks over criminal's shoulder.*)

BRUNO. I don't know why I did it . . . I mean . . . I was off duty and I see this guy ripping a camera off this other guy . . . So I nab him . . . Then I start feeling sorry for him . . . what the hell . . . I'm off duty . . . What am I . . . a gung ho cop or something . . . and then I see these other cops closing in . . . and the guy looks so orphany . . . I don't know.

GOYA. He's welcome. Anybody that can stand five feet away from the stool and hit the bowl smack dab in the center is welcome . . . (GOYA *shuts door, and leans up against the wall between Gramp's room and the bath, arms outstreched.*) They're coming at me from all sides . . . two in the bathroom, one next door to the bathroom, Germans, cops . . . and the day is still young. ([*Sound cue 17.*] *Toilet flushes, and* GOYA *slides to floor; she peeks through the keyhole.*) Hmmm . . . looks Chinese . . . never had a Chinese man before . . . at least not such a young one . . . at least not recently. Let me see, got to figure things out. (*Takes a swig.*) Sylvia gets Bruno . . . Adolph gets arrested . . . Mario gets buried . . . and I get the Chinese. I must be tired . . . It's working out too well. (*Takes a swig.*) And who gets Grampa . . . I must be tired . . . It's not working out at all. ([*Sound cue 18.*])

(BLACKOUT.)

(Goya *starts for stairs on FA, then in blackout goes to bath door. Criminal enters then she exits. Criminal attaches himself to the radiator.*)

ACT ONE

Scene 3

Same as before. It's late at night and the lighting of the stage is such as to indicate that people have gone to bed. The booze bottle is on the table where Goya *left it. Sitting in a chair . . . handcuffed to the radiator is the* Criminal. *He's asleep. The front door opens and in comes* Mario *on his tiptoes . . . he's a little drunk. Hiccups. Takes in an enormous quantity of air and holds it in order to get rid of the hiccups. Sees the bottle of booze on the table and exhales. Does not see the* Criminal. *Goes toward the bottle.*

Mario. I run away from the bottle and the bottle runs after me . . . It's like in one of them fairy tales. (*He walks toward the bottle.*) According to an article in Outdoor Life kids who were bottle fed never outgrow their desire for the bottle . . . or two. The question is . . . If I were breast fed would I see a breast sitting on the dining room table. (*Takes bottle. Looks at it. Sniffs it.*) This is German booze . . . Adolf's been here. Poor guy . . . Goya wouldn't have him if he was the last man on earth. Yes, she would . . . If he was dead last . . . I think she'd like that . . . to have the very last man on earth . . . (*Takes a swig.*) She'd like it even better if she had the first man on earth . . . (*Takes a swig.*) And a whole bunch in between. (*Ready to take another swig . . . sees the* Criminal *handcuffed to the radiator. Stops. Looks at the bottle. Looks at the* Criminal. *Goes over to him.*) Are you here about the ad? Hmmm? Poor soul.

Looks exhausted. Probably rushed right over when he read the thing . . . just like I did . . . I couldn't believe I finally saw a position advertised for which I qualified. WANTED—A MAN. That's all. A man. (*Looks at the* CRIMINAL.) He looks kind of young, though. But, Goya likes young men. (*Takes a swig.*) And she likes old men. And those that aren't so old or so young. (*Takes another good look at the* CRIMINAL.) The thing is . . . he looks Chinese to me . . . or Japanese. Must be Japanese. He has that Japanese look. Plus he's got that camera . . . in short . . . a Jap. Or a Chinaman that looks like a Jap. He probably carried that camera to make everybody think he's not Chinese. (*To the* CRIMINAL.) Not that it matters one bit. Goya likes Chinese men . . . and Japanese men. (*Takes a swig.*) And Arabs . . . and Viet Cong . . . and tall Swedes and short-legged Serbians. (*To the* CRIMINAL.) She once told me that Indians make good husbands. And Greeks . . . and Portuguese fishermen. And Montenegran peasants . . . or was it Lithuanian peasants? Not that it matters. I mean I wouldn't sweat it if you were Lithuanian. You won't believe this . . . (*Takes a swig.*) They had an article in National Geographics about this tribe of people that was discovered living in caves . . . living in prehistoric conditions . . . You get the picture . . . prehistoric cavemen . . . And you know what Goya said . . . You guessed it . . . Cavemen, she said, probably make very nice husbands. And the damn thing was that National Geographics went on to verify her statement in the next issue . . . I guess they took a poll of prehistoric cave wives and they said they preferred prehistoric cave husbands nine to one. What I'm trying to say is . . . you have a good solid chance . . . as long as you're not a fag or a German . . . or heaven forbid, a combination of the two. (*Takes a good hard look at the criminal.*) Wait a minute . . . Maybe the poor guy's German . . . That must be it . . . Poor thing . . . He found out Goya hates Germans and he tried to pass himself off as a Chinaman . . . She'll see right through him. You're wasting your time buddy. Come clean . . . what is your nationality, Herr Suitor. (*Shakes him.*) Verstehen sie mich? (*Shakes him.* CRIMINAL *opens his eyes with difficulty.*)

CRIMINAL. Hey . . .

MARIO. You speak English, I see. Your nationality, my good man, what is your nationality?

CRIMINAL. I'm an American. (MARIO *sighs with total incredulity. The criminal is either totally exhausted or very sleepy . . . shuts his eyes again.*)

MARIO. I find it amazing . . . truly amazing . . . you see some character and you can tell a mile off he's from Hong Kong or some such Kong and he swears to you he's American . . . While this New England dude whose father not only came over on the Mayflower but built the damn thing as well gets his kicks by trying to peddle himself off as a direct descendant of Taras Bulba or some other bulba like that . . . Makes no sense . . . Right? Hmmm? (*He looks at criminal. Sees the handcuffs.*) Christ . . . she's got him handcuffed. Must want to keep him then and if she wants to keep him he's not German. What the hell is he then? Must be a Jap just as I thought. (*Walks toward couch, the one with the back facing the audience.*) Not that it matters. (*Lies down on the couch and disappears from view. His head reappears again as he looks at the criminal.*) Oh, it matters to some all right . . . but not to Goya . . . and that's what matters. (*His head disappears from view. A hiccup is heard . . . and then the beginning of a snore and then nothing.*)

a fresh supply . . . yes . . . she's a real modern convenience, my mother . . . that's why I turned to a life of crime . . . I mean . . . it's better than no life at all . . . what I'm trying to say is . . . it's all my mother's fault . . . You should have her handcuffed to this radiator . . . the old ice bag . . . Ah . . . nobody gives a damn about me . . . (SYLVIA *looks at the* CRIMINAL. BRUNO *looks at* SYLVIA *looking at the* CRIMINAL. CRIMINAL *looks at* SYLVIA.)

BRUNO. Want to sit down or something?

SYLVIA. No, thanks. (SYLVIA *sits down at the table. Looks at* CRIMINAL. BRUNO *stands frozen.*)

BRUNO. Look here, Sylvia. . . . Pretty soon I'm going to start talking . . . It'll be any second now . . . If you don't want me to start say so . . . but once I start I won't be able to stop.

SYLVIA. What is it . . . a speech or something?

BRUNO. Something like that . . . You don't want to hear, right?

SYLVIA. Why not . . . I'll listen.

BRUNO. Because you've got nothing better to do, right?

SYLVIA. No . . . I've got things to do.

BRUNO. Am I keeping you from something?

SYLVIA. I'll listen already.

CRIMINAL. Me, too.

BRUNO. You see, Sylvia . . . you're always coming and going . . . I held that against you for a long time . . . because I'd like to be able to come and go myself.

CRIMINAL. That makes two of us.

BRUNO. But I can't. You see this is your home . . . Goya's your mother . . . you take it for granted . . . you take it for granted that you're my sister and that I'm your brother and really nothing's further from the truth . . . I'm an orphan, Sylvia . . .

SYLVIA. Since when.

BRUNO. Ever since they put me in the orphanage and up to the time Goya adopted me . . .

SYLVIA. Adopted?

BRUNO. Yes, I'm an adopted orphan, Sylvia.

SYLVIA. But mother never said . . .

BRUNO. To her it doesn't matter. To Mario it doesn't matter. It shouldn't really matter to me.

SYLVIA. But it does matter.

BRUNO. Yes, it does.

SYLVIA. Don't say another word, Bruno . . . I understand.

BRUNO. I have to say more. I told you before it's a whole speech.

SYLVIA. Oh, Bruno . . . how you must hate me . . . me . . . their real child and you an orphan . . . the envy and jealousy that must have filled your formative years . . . the scars you must carry.

CRIMINAL. Let him speak, eh?

SYLVIA. Is that why you became a cop . . . to get even with the world . . . Oh, Bruno . . . don't say another word.

BRUNO. Hold it, Sylvia! It all sounds good, but hold it. Let me continue . . . I don't know how old I was when they put in the orphanage . . . not very . . . and the first time I heard the word "orphan" I thought it was this guy's name. Billy Orphan. Then I found out that I was an orphan too, and I figured that Billy and I were related. Then I found out that we were all orphans . . . and I figured . . . hell . . . somebody must be lying . . . we can't all be relatives.

SYLVIA. I'm going to cry.

BRUNO. Later, Sylvia, please . . . let me finish. So we were all orphans but I still didn't know what the word meant except that we talked about everything in terms of that one word . . . the outside world was a non-orphanage . . . those that got placed were de-orphanated . . . those that came back were re-orphanated. For a long time I thought only boys were orphans . . . so when I grew up I wanted to be a girl. Then I found out that there were female orphans too . . . we called them orphenes. But I still didn't know what the word meant. So I asked one of the guards one day . . . what's an orphan? He said it was somebody that nobody liked. But these other orphans liked me . . . Billy liked me . . . so I asked him if that made me a non-orphan. He said no . . . He said being liked by another orphan didn't count.

SYLVIA. The beast! Don't say another . . .

BRUNO. Hold it, Sylvia! So I started thinking that nothing that happened in the orphanage counted. The only things that mattered happened on the outside. For the whole time that that I was there some police athletic league kept promising to take us to a ball game. We went to bed every night hoping that tomorrow was the big day when we'd go to a ball game. Hell, we didn't know what a ball game was . . . properly speaking . . . but it was on the outside so we assumed it was something incredible . . . something unheard of . . . and finally the big day came and this man took us all to a ball game.

SYLVIA. And what happened?

BRUNO. The Yankees won.

CRIMINAL. There's a shocker for you.

BRUNO. That was it. The Yankees won . . . And all of us orphans sat there scratching our ass thinking . . . You mean this is it . . . this is the real thing . . . That's why I still go to ball games . . . I figure one of these days I'm going to see it the way I thought it would be . . . you know . . . the ball game of the century . . . the ball game of all time . . .

CRIMINAL. Did you catch the Mets against the Cubs . . . there was a game for you.

BRUNO. And you know what? . . . when I go there I see some of those orphans I once knew . . . Billy's there every time . . . They're all grown up and everything but still looking orphany as hell . . . still waiting for the ball game . . . you see don't you . . . you see how we were tricked into thinking that the outside world was so exciting and full of wonders . . . not that we thought it was all good . . . but we did think it was full of extremes . . . that's it . . . extremes . . . . the most beautiful and the ugliest things were on the outside . . . nothing in between . . . the orphanage was in between . . . and that's why I became a cop.

CRIMINAL. I don't get the connection.

BRUNO. I thought that by being a cop I'd be able to find those extremes . . . and sometimes I think I'm close . . . Sometimes I'd be walking my beat and suddenly I hear this screaming . . . I mean screaming so painful your heart wants to commit suicide . . . and I think to myself . . . Hot dog! This is it! This is the saddest goddamned thing that ever happened in the world! And I rush to the house . . . I rush upstairs and what do I find . . . This old lady's screaming because her parakeet ate something foul and was vomiting all over the cage. (SYLVIA *laughs*.)

SYLVIA. It wasn't. (BRUNO *smiles*.)

BRUNO. Swear to God, Sylvie . . . that damned parakeet was barfing like a truck driver . . . the old lady screaming her head off . . . for some reason she turned a fan on it . . . there it was . . . birdbarf all over the wallpaper . . . (CRIMINAL *laughs too*. SYLVIA'S *laughing . . . doing an imitation of the barfing parakeet. She's standing now and in the course of her laughter and imitation she comes to lean on* BRUNO . . . *as if seeking support . . . The leaning turns into a hug but the laughter is still used as an excuse for the contact.* BRUNO *stiffens*.)

SYLVIA. Bruno . . . your story has touched my heart.

BRUNO. Has it, Sylvie . . . has it really?

SYLVIA. It has . . . it's touched it . . .

CRIMINAL. It was a touching story.

SYLVIA. You were forced by circumstances to love me as a sister. How you must have hated me for that.

BRUNO. No, Sylvia . . . I never hated you.

SYLVIA. I hated you because I thought you were my brother. I hate having to love because of traditional family ties. And now that it's too late, I see that I should have loved you all along like a brother I never had. We're in the same boat, you and I. We're brother and sister in spirit. You seek your happiness in the streets . . . I seek mine in the voting booths . . . Have you ever voted, Bruno?

BRUNO. No.

SYLVIA. You poor baby . . . you've lost faith in the electoral process.

BRUNO. No . . . it's kind of personal.

SYLVIA. Tell me, Bruno . . .

BRUNO. Something happens every time . . . I register and all . . . I go to vote . . . I wait in line . . . but when my turn comes I always have to go to the bathroom.

SYLVIA. Does that happen just in the national elections?

BRUNO. No . . . state elections . . . city . . . bond issues . . . I don't know what causes it.

SYLVIA. Maybe it's the thrill of being able to participate in a free democracy.

BRUNO. That must be it.

CRIMINAL. That's probably why the parakeet vomited too . . . from the thrill of it all.

SYLVIA. How I wish I was in a voting booth right now . . . and I saw your name on the ballot, Bruno . . . I'd vote for you . . . I'd pull that lever for you. Kiss me, Bruno.

CRIMINAL. Hey, now . . .

SYLVIA. Why don't you kiss me.

BRUNO. I'll tell you why not . . .

SYLVIA. Don't tell me . . . Why don't you just do it.

BRUNO. Because . . .

SYLVIA. Don't talk . . . What's there left to say.

BRUNO. One question at a time, Sylvia. My heart is pounding, Sylvia . . . It's going at least eighty-five a minute . . . Is yours pounding?

SYLVIA. It's pounding.

BRUNO. I got to be sure.

CRIMINAL. She said it's pounding.

BRUNO. I couldn't do it if your heart was strolling along at sixty-five beats . . . I've waited too long for something that counted . . . this has to be it.

SYLVIA. This is it. (BRUNO *grabs her. Kisses her.* [*Sound cue 20.*] *Outside the house* DODO *lets out a howl.*)

CRIMINAL. All I can say is hey . . . (BRUNO *picks her up.* SYLVIA *waves to the* CRIMINAL *as* BRUNO *carries her around looking for a place to put her down. Takes her to the couch. Drops her right on top of* MARIO. SYLVIA *lets out a scream.*)

SYLVIA. Upstairs, Bruno! Let's go upstairs! (*They run up the stairs as if they were on fire. Disappear inside one of the rooms.* DODO *lets out another howl.* OLD MAN *comes out of his room.*)

OLD MAN. SHUT UP! ALL OF YOU! (*Sees the* CRIMINAL.) Who the hell are you?

CRIMINAL. I'm the meter man. How about you, gramps?

OLD MAN. Gramps! (*The* OLD MAN, *without even thinking, flies at him, grabs him by the shirt and shakes him.*)

CRIMINAL. I'm handcuffed, dammit. Hey . . .

OLD MAN. You goddammit . . . you . . . goddamn you . . . I'll blast you. (*The* OLD MAN *lets go of the criminal's shirt . . . stomps to the chest of drawers. Opens drawer . . . pulls out a gun.*)

CRIMINAL. Hey . . . (*The* OLD MAN *puts gun back. Opens another drawer. Pulls out a portable typewriter. Carries it back to his room.*)

OLD MAN. I'll issue a written statement . . . I'll blast you. (*Goes into his room and slams the door shut. The door wakes up* MARIO. *His head appears above the couch back.*)

MARIO. Jesus . . . It feels like as if somebody sat on my head. (*Gets up. Typing is heard for the* OLD MAN's *room.*) I better go to bed. (*Sees the* CRIMINAL.) You still here? (CRIMINAL *is ready to cry.*)

CRIMINAL. Am I still here? No . . . not all here. I don't think anybody here is all here . . . or all there for that matter.

MARIO. Well . . . I'm going to bed. (*Starts going.*)

CRIMINAL. HOLD IT! JUST HOLD IT RIGHT

THERE! I want some goddamned recognition . . . Did you know that I'm dangerous criminal?

MARIO. Sometimes I feel like a criminal myself. You probably feel like that all the time, eh?

CRIMINAL. It's useless . . .

MARIO. No, don't feel useless. You shouldn't. Criminals have their place in a society . . . With all due respect to Bruno . . . I shudder to think what cops would do to decent citizens out of sheer boredom if it wasn't for criminals . . . Keep them busy, my boy . . . I know it's a rotten job but somebody has to do it . . .

CRIMINAL. I'm going to sue somebody. I'll need psychiatric help after all this is over . . . Wait . . . don't go . . . I got news for you . . . Did you know that the cop who lives here is an orphan . . . did you know that?

MARIO. Did you know that I'm an orphan too?

CRIMINAL. No.

MARIO. Well, I am . . . I don't even know what my nationality is. That's why Goya loves me, I think . . . (*Walks upstairs.*) One night I'm a Portuguese fisherman . . . another a prehistoric caveman . . . shortlegged Serbian . . . Fat Finn . . . Greek Orthodox . . . Agnostic Albanian. Catholic . . . Buddhist . . . Monk. (*Mutters his way up the stairs and disappears inside his room.*)

CRIMINAL. The thing to do is remain casual . . . Agnostic Albanian? . . . All right! And that girl . . . I thought she was giving me the eye, and then she runs off with that orphan. An orphan beats me out . . . A cop orphan! It's sort of like being at home . . . I'm sitting downstairs wondering what the hell I'm doing here. (GOYA *enters; puts coat on rack.*)

GOYA. Well . . . he's not at the bookstore . . . and it looks like rain . . . Where is everybody?

CRIMINAL. Lady . . . I don't even know who everybody is.

GOYA. Mario didn't come while I was gone?

CRIMINAL. Nobody came but a whole bunch of people went. (*She hears typing.*)

GOYA. Who's typing?

CRIMINAL. The old man. He said he's going to blast us.

GOYA. What did you do . . . call him gramps or somethings?

CRIMINAL. Yeah.

GOYA. That was diplomatic of you.

CRIMINAL. I didn't know . . . Good God . . . why am I explaining myself . . . Look . . . I want a lawyer.

GOYA. Can you afford a lawyer?

CRIMINAL. Damn right, I can.

GOYA. Then you don't need one. I'm going to bed.

CRIMINAL. Hold it! Don't go. I've got news for you . . . Did you know there are two orphans in this house?

GOYA. Is that counting me or not?

CRIMINAL. No.

GOYA. Then you better make it three.

CRIMINAL. You too . . . you mean nobody here knows who his parents are?

GOYA. No, do you?

CRIMINAL. Of course I do.

GOYA. You criminals think you know everything.

CRIMINAL. I even know who my grandparents are.

GOYA. You must have ben adopted when you were very young.

CRIMINAL. I wasn't adopted.

GOYA. I can see why not . . . who would want to adopt a liar like you.

CRIMINAL. I didn't need to be adopted . . . My mother had me and my mother kept me.

GOYA. Sure, sure . . .

CRIMINAL. If you don't believe me, call her. 388-4575. (GOYA *dials the number*.) and tell her to come and get me. If a man's voice answers . . . that's my mother.

GOYA. There's no answer.

CRIMINAL. My mother's deaf. Let it ring.

GOYA. Hello . . . hate to wake you up . . . I'm calling from the League of Women Voters and I'm taking a survey . . . Do you have a natural born son who's a criminal? You don't. Thank you. (*Hangs up.*) Now you know the truth.

CRIMINAL. She doesn't know I'm a criminal.

GOYA. I know . . . Bruno knows . . . Sylvia knows . . . and the old man probably knows . . . but your mother doesn't know. Common.

CRIMINAL. She doesn't want to know. If she was a real mother . . .

GOYA. Aha . . . if she was a real mother.

CRIMINAL. She's not as real as she could be.

GOYA. I think I see your problem. You think you're a real son but you have a mother who's not . . . That, my friend, makes you an orphan.

CRIMINAL. All I'm trying to say is that she's a cold-hearted bitch of a real mother.

GOYA. I don't know about that . . . I mean . . . I only talked to her once . . . she seemed like a decent woman to me . . .

CRIMINAL. It's useless . . .

GOYA. Don't feel useless. You criminals are our best deterrent to crime . . . I mean . . . look at you . . . You look so miserable in your chosen field . . . Cheer up, . . . I've got plans for you . . .

CRIMINAL. I've got plans of my own.

GOYA. Well, change them, I've changed mine often enough. Goodnight. (*She goes up stairs—at top* CRIMINAL *speaks.*)

CRIMINAL. Goodnight. (*As she disappears, after a beat, the hall lights turn off. After another beat we hear.*)

GOYA. MARIO, YOU SONOVABITCH . . . WHERE WERE YOU!

CRIMINAL. Oh, so that's Mario. Slowly but surely I'm finding my way around here. It's a club. If you're an orphan, you go upstairs and roll around in bed . . . if you're not . . . they handcuff you to the radiator.

END OF ACT ONE

ACT TWO

Scene 1

Same as before. [Sound cue 21.] It's later on in the night. The CRIMINAL is asleep on the floor. SYLVIA appears at the top of the stairway. She's wearing a flimsy nothing. She tiptoes carefully down the stairs . . . Stops in front of the CRIMINAL. Looks at him from various angles. Coughs, trying to get his attention. He's asleep. She sighs louder. He's still asleep. SYLVIA walks past him and kicks on his head.

SYLVIA. Excuse me. (*A* CRIMINAL *snore comes as a reply.* SYLVIA *comes back. Stops in front of him. Kicks him again.*) Excuse me. (SYLVIA *gets impatient. She stands there and begins kicking his head, timing her kicks to the rhythm of her apologies.*) Excuseme—excuseme—excuseme . . . (*The* CRIMINAL *is rudely awakened.* SYLVIA *backs off. Pretends she hardly notices him.*)

CRIMINAL. Oh God! What a nightmare.

SYLVIA. I couldn't sleep.

CRIMINAL. Me neither . . . But that's nothing new to me . . . When you're running from the law you learn to make do without sleep . . . It's like war . . . You develop cat reflexes . . . I could be sound asleep and hear a pin drop and wake up just like that. Like a cat.

SYLVIA. Yeah . . . some dead cat. I almost broke my foot trying to wake you up. Why did you steal that camera.

CRIMINAL. I wanted to take my mother's picture. Nobody believes me when I say she looks like Johnny Unitas.

SYLVIA. You could have bought it . . . you didn't have to steal.

CRIMINAL. I tried . . . I looked in all the stores but none of them carried my mother's picture.

SYLVIA. I don't think that's funny.

CRIMINAL. Chinese aren't known for their sense of humor.

SYLVIA. Are you Chinese?

CRIMINAL. No . . . but my sense of humor is . . . I'm Japanese.

SYLVIA. I don't think that's funny.

CRIMINAL. What do you expect from a Jap? With my background . . . family life and gene composition I consider myself lucky to be able to laugh at other people's jokes . . . You know what my mother's favorite game is . . . we play Mt. Rushmore . . . we sit and stare and try to look majestic . . . a majestic Jap family . . . you could spill a bowl of hot pea soup on my mother's face and if you didn't say excuse me, she wouldn't notice. Every now and then she'd turn to my dad and say . . . did you say something. And he'd whimper, No, should I have.

SYLVIA. I thought Japanese were supposed to have a very nice family life.

CRIMINAL. Maybe in Japan they do. Do you realize that my grandparents, on my mother's side, were at Hiroshima when the bomb fell . . . and they survived . . . survived nothing . . . I think the radiation actually perked them up a bit. Taking all this into account can you honestly blame me for becoming a criminal? Don't you want to shake my hand and say well done?

SYLVIA. What kind of a criminal are you?

CRIMINAL. I became a criminal so I wouldn't have to answer questions like that . . . Where do you work . . . How much do you make . . . All right . . . Let's say I'm a freelance criminal . . . Although the part about the free is in doubt right now. (GOYA *appears at the top of the stairway. Sits down and listens, reacting every now and then to something* SYLVIA *says.*)

Sylvia. Did you ever rape anybody? (Goya *slaps her forehead.*)

Criminal. Rape? Me? I have my pride, you know . . . I don't have to rape . . . I can pay for it.

Sylvia. You must have thought about it . . . I mean . . . just in case the opportunity presented itself . . . You must have worked out some plan.

Criminal. All right. Here's my plan . . . I'd pull out my gun and say . . . Hey, this is a rape.

Sylvia. And then what?

Criminal. And then I'd shoot myself in the head. I have my pride, you know.

Sylvia. Have you ever thought about reforming?

Criminal. Yeah . . . my mother . . . But I never got anywhere.

Sylvia. Goya says reformed criminals make good husbands.

Criminal. Not if they're Japanese they don't.

Sylvia. I've heard Japanese men make good lovers.

Criminal. Yeah, out of plastic.

Sylvia. I saw the way you were looking at me.

Criminal. It's a free country.

Sylvia. I couldn't sleep. It upset me the way you were looking at me. You had the same stinking look my husband had before we were married . . .

Criminal. Oh, I didn't know you . . .

Sylvia. I'm divorced now . . . Divorced! As if what we had was a marriage in the first place. The first date I had with that beast . . . you know what he told me . . . he said . . . all I have to do is get one of my hands on your tits and I'll have you under my control . . . and that's what you're thinking . . . You men are all alike . . . You think tits are control panels on a car or something . . . press a button and the heat comes on . . . Well, I've got news for you . . . It doesn't work . . . not on this girl . . . Go ahead . . . try your luck buster. (*She offers one of her breasts to his free hand.*) What's the matter . . . afraid. Common . . . I'd like to shatter this myth once and for all. (*The* CRIMINAL *considers and finally gives in . . . Fondles her breast somewhat mechanically.*) You see . . . nothing.

CRIMINAL. That's not my good hand. I'm a southpaw.

SYLVIA. You want to kiss me. You think that'll do it . . . It won't . . .

CRIMINAL. You've got a helluva way of proving people wrong. What did you do . . . Marry that guy just to prove to him he'd make a rotten husband.

SYLVIA. Don't talk about him . . . I'm trying to forget.

CRIMINAL. How about that huge orphan upstairs . . . Did you forget about him too?

SYLVIA. Bruno . . . dear, gentle Bruno . . . I did think for a minute . . . but no . . . he deserves somebody better than myself.

CRIMINAL. And I don't.

SYLVIA. No.

CRIMINAL. So I don't.

SYLVIA. I'm really no better than you. Sometimes I feel like a criminal myself.

CRIMINAL. I feel like a criminal all the time, I mean . . . I had a steady job and I felt like a criminal . . . I worked for the Department of Welfare . . . If you think I'm a criminal now you should have seen me then . . . so what happens . . . Republicans cut back on Welfare and I lose my job.

SYLVIA. I did it. I brought the Republicans to power . . . and there you stand . . . a victim of my vote . . . How you must hate me.

CRIMINAL. I voted for the Republicans too . . . straight ticket.

SYLVIA. You didn't.

CRIMINAL. The hell I didn't. I still have nightmares about it.

SYLVIA. But why?

CRIMINAL. I got tired of being a good boy. I did it to spite my mother. That was my first criminal act.

SYLVIA. And I did it to spite my husband.

CRIMINAL. We really showed them, eh?

SYLVIA. We're in the same boat you and I . . . seeking our happiness in the turbulent sea of forgetfulness . . . All those poor people on fixed incomes . . . How will we ever make it up to them . . . We'll try won't we? We'll have to try. We'll get a fresh start. You'll get your job back and I'll do charity work. We're still young . . . we have many important elections ahead of us. We can do it.

CRIMINAL. Not handcuffed to the radiator we can't.

SYLVIA. I'll set you free . . . we'll wait till Bruno goes to work.

CRIMINAL. What if he takes me to the station with him? (GOYA *gets up and disappears into her room.*)

SYLVIA. He won't. He says he doesn't know what to do with you. But I do. (*Kisses him.*) You're so warm.

CRIMINAL. That's a funny thing about me. Handcuff me to a radiator for a few hours and I get warm.

SYLVIA. I can see us already . . . We'll have little biracial babies . . . and we'll adopt kids . . . We'll adopt more kids than Goya ever dreamed of adopting . . . and who knows . . . they might even write a story about us in some magazine or something . . . Oh, I'm going back to bed to dream about it all . . . Good night.

CRIMINAL. Good night. (SYLVIA *goes up the stairway . . . blows him a kiss and disappears.*) Biracial babies! Well, I'll be damned . . . I think I'm looking forward to the whole thing . . . I can hear myself already . . . Hey, there kid . . . I'm your daddy, hey . . .

(BLACKOUT.)

ACT TWO

Scene 2

The clock chimes in the darkness, [Sound cue 22.] **then morning light comes up.** GOYA *is discovered fixing her hair on the stairs.*

GOYA. Sleep well?

CRIMINAL. Not bad.

GOYA. Glad to hear it . . . "Mr. Southpaw!"

CRIMINAL. Oh dear . . .

GOYA. So . . . you've got plans of your own, eh? Biracial babies, eh? You want to take my only child away from me?

CRIMINAL. Look lady, I don't know what Sylvia told you . . .

GOYA. She didn't tell me anything . . . and I can sense things . . . and I can sense that when Bruno comes down here shortly . . .

CRIMINAL. Oh look lady . . . don't tell Bruno . . .

GOYA. You let me handle this, you hear . . . You so much as open your mouth, and it's "goodbye Charlie!" (BRUNO *appears upstairs; he is fully dressed and whistles as he comes down the stairs.*) Is that you, Bruno? I can't see . . . I forgot my glasses upstairs.

BRUNO. You don't wear glasses.

GOYA. No, but I should. Old age is catching up with me.

BRUNO. I guess you're wondering why I didn't wait up for you last night.

GOYA. Speak up son. You're looking good . . . from what I can see.

BRUNO. I feel good, ma. (*Guilty.*) I mean . . . I'm sorry I didn't wait up, but you see . . .

GOYA. That's all right. No need to apologize. You felt sleepy and went to bed.

BRUNO. That's just it, ma . . . I wasn't sleepy . . . Things happened that I never . . .

GOYA. Oh, poor Mario.

BRUNO. Yeah. How is Dad?

GOYA. Don't ask . . . He's breathing his last if he's breathing at all. You're looking at a widow in the making, Bruno. (*Pretends to cry.*)

BRUNO. Didn't he pull this once before.

GOYA. I can't remember . . . my memory's fading . . . Oh, Mario . . . Mario . . . Do you know he tried to convince me he's German so I wouldn't be heartbroken when he dies . . .

BRUNO. Maybe we should call a doctor.

GOYA. He said he went to a doctor yesterday . . . Read all the magazines in the waiting room and left sicker than when he came in . . .

BRUNO. I know this is no time to bring up what I have to say . . . But you see . . . Last night . . . when I told Sylvia . . .

GOYA. Better tell me tonight, Bruno . . . I can't concentrate . . . My head's full of worries . . .

BRUNO. But you see, Sylvia and I . . .

GOYA. Oh, Mario, Mario . . . I'll be like a little lost lamb without you . . .

BRUNO. O.K. Ma . . . we'll talk tonight. (*Feels his pockets.*) I don't know what I did with my keys. I'd like to take him down to the station. Get him out of your way.

GOYA. Leave him. It helps a little to see a creature more miserable than I.

BRUNO. O.K. I'll see you tonight, Ma. Call me at the station if anything happens. (BRUNO *exits.*)

GOYA. I will son . . . I will. Now where were we?

CRIMINAL. Look, I've had a rough time of it, lady. It feels like I've been sitting next to this radiator for years. My scalp's all dried out and I'm getting dandruff . . . the transition from my home where we don't even believe in warmth hardly heat is too great . . . I'll tell you honestly. I've been trying to get arrested for a few months. I thought prison life would suit me . . . no gas bills . . . no rent . . . no worries . . . I even thought my folks might thaw out a bit if they had to come and visit me . . . I know it sounds absurd . . . I mean . . . I've only talked to Sylvia a few minutes . . . but she seems better than prison . . . as a matter of fact she seems better than most things I've run into.

GOYA. You must have had a rough time of it. Goodness . . . do all you Chinese talk so much?

CRIMINAL. I'm Japanese.

GOYA. That's right. I forgot about the camera.

CRIMINAL. ALL JAPANESE DON'T HAVE CAMERAS!

GOYA. Don't get in a huff . . . Gracious . . .

CRIMINAL. I'm tired of having people think that every Jap they see is some kind of trained Polaroid bear that knows everything about cameras . . . Perfect strangers stop me in the street and ask my advice about filters . . . why their shutter is getting stuck . . . The only reason I stole this camera is because another Jap was carrying it . . . I can't stand to see another Jap with another goddamned camera.

GOYA. I know how you feel . . . They all have them.

CRIMINAL. It's useless . . .

GOYA. Don't feel useless . . . A young man your age. Lord, oh, Lord . . . do you realize that you're going to make me a grandmother? I don't know if I can't take it. I'll probably become like that old man over there . . . DON'T CALL ME GRANDMOTHER. I'LL BLAST YOU . . . I just hope I don't start resorting to cosmetics to recapture my youth . . . dying my hair grandmother red . . . plucking my eyebrows and painting on new ones . . . Tell me the truth . . . I don't look like the type to pluck eyebrows, do I?

CRIMINAL. Your own . . . no. (GOYA *laughs*.)

GOYA. Goddamn you kids . . . you're all criminals.

([*Sounds cue 23 and 24.*] *Thunder is heard outside.*)
Poor Dodo . . . he's going to get soaked. (*Doorbell rings.* GOYA *primps ever so slightly and opens the door. A* MAN *steps inside, umbrella first . . . a ragged-looking newspaper in the other hand. Hereafter, until his baptismal, he'll be known as* CLIENT.)

CLIENT. I'm here about the ad . . . Are you . . .

GOYA. Yes, I'm the ad . . . Shut your umbrella, please . . . It's bad luck inside a house. (*The* CLIENT *shuts the umbrella with difficulty. He is nervous and shaking half from the chill of the rain, half from nerves. Enters and sees the* CRIMINAL.)

CLIENT. Hello.

CRIMINAL. Hey!

GOYA. Sit down. (CLIENT *sits down in armchair.*) Coffee? (CLIENT *simply hold out his hands.* GOYA *crosses to kitchen and returns with pot, hot mat and cup and saucer. Fills cup very full.* CLIENT'S *hands shake so that he spills coffee all over himself. He puts empty cup down on the table.*) Want some more?

CLIENT. No . . . not really. (CLIENT *looks at* CRIMINAL.)

GOYA. Well?

CLIENT. Oh . . . am I next?

GOYA. Yes. A German came, but I turned him down.

CLIENT. German?

GOYA. You're not German, are you?

CLIENT. No . . . not really.

GOYA. Good . . . then we're all set.

CLIENT. (*Looking at* CRIMINAL.) I feel a little odd.

GOYA. You look a little wet.

CLIENT. It's raining.

GOYA. Nothing odd about that.

CLIENT. No . . . not really. It always rains when I go out.

GOYA. Good, then you must be used to it.

CLIENT. Yes . . . I suppose, (*Looks at* CRIMINAL.) only I still feel a little odd.

Goya. Oh . . . I see . . . Don't worry, he's handcuffed. (Criminal *picks up handcuffed hand to show.*)

Client. A relative?

Goya. No. Not yet . . . he's a criminal.

Client. Nice house. (*Looking at* Criminal.) Steam heat I see.

Goya. You cold or something?

Client. (*Looks at* Criminal.) Oh no . . . not really.

Goya. I mean if you're cold . . .

Client. Nein! No I'm not.

Goya. You're awfully jittery.

Client. Only when I'm warm.

Goya. Could you cool down a bit?

Client. I'm not sure. Excuse me for asking, but are you the woman who put the ad in the paper?

Goya. No . . . my husband did.

Client. Where's your husband?

Goya. Upstairs.

Client. (*Looks at* Criminal . . . *then at* Goya . . . *then at ad . . . then full front.*) I don't understand a thing . . . it always happens to me . . . A moment always comes when I don't understand a thing . . . and this is that moment again.

Goya. What don't you understand?

Client. Not a thing.

Goya. Common, don't be a hog.

Client. Why's the ad in the paper?

Goya. Because my husband might die any day.

Client. I'm sorry.

Goya. I'll tell him. So, if he dies I'd like to find somebody to take his place.

Client. That's horrible . . . The man's not even dead and you . . .

Goya. If he were dead you wouldn't be here talking to me . . . I'd have found somebody by now.

Client. Oh, and I'm supposed to be thrilled to death that I'm here talking with you.

Goya. Look here . . . it's raining out there . . . it's

dry and warm in here . . . there's muggers and killers and rapists out there . . . you could be mugged, killed and raped . . . and wet on top of it . . . be glad you're in here.

CLIENT. Glad? With that criminal sitting over there.

GOYA. We keep our criminals handcuffed.

CLIENT. So what do you want me to say . . . that I'm glad I'm here. All right. I'm glad. It's warm. The coffee smells nice . . . I'm talking with a woman . . . I haven't talked with a woman in years it seems like . . . All right, I'm glad. It's nice. It's lovely. I'm even getting to like that criminal over there. Everything's fantastic . . . and now I'm going to get turned down.

GOYA. Don't be so sure of yourself.

CLIENT. It never fails. If it's nice . . . I get turned down. If it's horrible and I hate it . . . I get an offer. Always has been and always will be. (*The door opens on the* OLD MAN'S *room and the* OLD MAN *comes out holding a sheet of paper in his hand. He waits a second as if challenging anyone to say something and then goes to the bathroom.*) Who's that?

GOYA. An old man . . . he answered the ad some years ago . . . but I couldn't . . . I mean he was too old to be my husband . . . so I offered him a nice position . . . to be my grandfather (OLD MAN *comes out*.) . . . well . . . he's been thinking it over.

CLIENT. Grandfather?

GOYA. Now you did it. (*The* OLD MAN *was just waiting for this. Takes a few steps forward. Holds out his written statement and half reads from the paper . . . half from his head.*)

OLD MAN. Once and for all I would like to clarify this misunderstanding. I know what you're up to . . . Yes . . . You want me to become your grandfather, which is to say a relative, so that you can treat me like people treat all their relatives . . . which is to say, like dirt. I know all about relatives. You'll pretend you understand me . . . You'll get a fixed idea of my role in the family and forget that I'm a man . . . You'll sneer when I do something that grandfathers aren't supposed to do or be disappointed if I don't do something grandfatherly every goddamned day of the week . . . Well . . . I refuse. I couldn't take the pressure. Ever since I can remember I was a man . . . nothing more . . . one of those men you see through the window in the street . . . a man who sometimes pees in the street . . . grandfathers don't do that . . . a man who sometimes looks through his wallet at pictures that have nothing to do with grandchildren or grand anything . . . There's nothing grand about me and never will be . . . So I refuse . . . Do you hear me. I spit on your offer. (*Stops. Seems ready to leave.*) BUT . . . and this is only in case of emergency . . . IF . . . and only IF you sometimes wake up in the middle of the night and feel *YOU* just have to have a grandfather . . . simply have to or your heart will break . . . then . . . I'll think about it. (*Goes back to his room slowly.* GOYA'S *touched but does her best not to show it.*)

GOYA. I do believe he's meliorating. How where were we?

CLIENT. You were about to give me the boot.

GOYA. What's the matter with you. I have all kinds of openings. Look . . . if Mario lives . . . that's my husband . . . if he lives . . . husband's out of the question. But you could be my uncle if you want . . . or brother . . . or my brother's distant cousin . . . depending on how close you want to get.

CLIENT. Is your uncle sick?

GOYA. What uncle?

CLIENT. Let's say I want to be your goddamned uncle. Do I have to wait for him to die too.

GOYA. No . . . we're presently all out of uncles. (CLIENT *thinks.*)

CLIENT. What else is available?

GOYA. Oh, now you're getting choosy on me.

CLIENT. I hate to jump at the first offer.

GOYA. There's no jumping . . . You walk in or you walk out . . . no jumping.

CLIENT. What about your brother?

GOYA. Don't have one.

CLIENT. Now you do. I'll be your goddamned brother. Why not. I don't have a sister or nothing . . . I don't have nothing . . .

GOYA. You're a nice looking man, you know.

CLIENT. Thanks, sis.

GOYA. Not too young—mature sort of—the gray in your hair goes well with the gray in mine . . . so you become my brother . . . Well, what happens if Mario dies . . . You know what happens . . . You stay my brother . . . I couldn't take the psychological trauma of marrying my own brother . . . in short . . . as a brother your chances of promotion are nil . . . but as a distant cousin . . .

CLIENT. I'll take it. I got nobody . . . no relatives . . . no friends . . . I'll take it. Please.

GOYA. Look, you don't have to shout, cuz. It's yours. I'll have an empty room shortly . . . bring your things over.

CLIENT. What things . . . I got no things . . . no relatives . . . no friends . . .

GOYA. Good. You can save yourself a trip. Just go upstairs . . . lie down and think about it for a while . . . make sure you know what you're doing . . . SYLVIA! It's the room with a slip hanging on the door knob . . . SYLVIA! (SYLVIA *comes out of the door as the* CLIENT *opens it. They nod at each other.* SYLVIA'S *carrying a suitcase. She comes down stairs.*)

SYLVIA. (*Puts suitcase* S. L. *of armchair.*) Oh, mother, have I got things to tell you.

GOYA. Why don't you write me a letter, dear. You never write, you know.

SYLVIA. I will. I'll write you mother . . . I can't wait to write you how well I'm doing . . . how happy I am.

GOYA. I can't wait to hear. I mean that— (*Rises, cross-*

ing to SYLVIA—*kiss on mouth, then embrace.*) Well . . . you better get started then, eh? Now why don't you unshackle that poor thing before he starts smoking. (SYLVIA *takes off the handcuffs from the* CRIMINAL.)

CRIMINAL. Hey . . . nice to be free again. (GOYA *opens front door, gets umbrella.*)

GOYA. That's what you think. Bruno comes home for lunch sometimes . . . so the two of you better hurry . . . there . . . take the umbrella . . . Oh, yeah . . . leave the stolen goods here . . . (*She takes the camera from the* CRIMINAL. *Examines it.*) Well . . . let's have something bordering on a smile. (SYLVIA *and* CRIMINAL *pose . . . huge smile.*) It's not that funny . . . never mind . . . hold it. (*Presses shutter.*) Now out into the rain with you. Some day when I'm old and gray and all alone . . . I'll blackmail you with this picture. (*The* CRIMINAL *wants to say something.*) Sayonara. (*The two of them leave hurriedly arm in arm.* CRIMINAL *reopens door.*)

CRIMINAL. Hey! (*Exits.*)

GOYA. (*Stands still.*) She took my suitcase. (*Goes to the window.*) Hand in hand . . . I knew it . . . I knew they'd dump that umbrella in the trash can. Just as I thought . . . She left me Dodo. (*Rises from sofa, crosses to the door, and aims camera.*) Common, Dodo . . . put your best leg forward, boy. ([*Sound cue 25.*])

(*The lights fade to black; as they come up,* GOYA *is discovered cleaning the kitchen table.* BRUNO *enters with umbrella, and places it* U. S. *end of sofa.*)

GOYA. You home for lunch?

BRUNO. (*Starting up stairs.*) No . . . not this time. (*Halfway up stairs he stops.*) Some coffee would be nice. (*Sees* MARIO *coming out of his room, then exits into his.* MARIO *descends stairs, sleepy and hung over. Remembers* DODO *and looks through curtain on front door. Goes out onto porch and we hear* DODO *barking happily,* [*Sound cue 26.*] MARIO *re-enters much happier and sits at kitchen table.*)

ACT TWO

SCENE 3

Same as before. GOYA *and* MARIO *are sitting at the table drinking coffee. They hear heavy footsteps above them. They look upstairs and continue drinking coffee. More footsteps. Sound of drawers being opened and shut.* BRUNO *appears at the top of the stairway carrying a suitcase. He's dressed in civilian clothes. He comes down the stairway in his usual heavy fashion . . . then . . . midway . . . as if changing his mind . . . he walks down steps normally, puts suitcase down near door and crosses to kitchen table.*

GOYA. You got everything?

BRUNO. I guess.

GOYA. I wouldn't feel too bad about Sylvia if I were you.

BRUNO. I don't, Ma . . . I was just going to use her as an excuse to leave . . . I get into awful ruts you know . . . When I was an orphan I was a hundred percent orphan . . . and then I became a hundred percent cop. Offhand, I suspect there's a helluva lot more to life than being a cop or an orphan. And I think I've been your son long enough . . . When I come back I'd like to come back as a friend.

GOYA. Now you're talking. I've got all the relatives I can use and not a single friend . . .

BRUNO. How about a kiss.

GOYA. How about a whole bunch. (*She goes up to him and kisses him all over.*) You ought to leave more often.

(*Kisses him some more.* MARIO *stands up and coughs.* BRUNO *comes over to him and hugs him. They kiss. Then* BRUNO *gets his suitcase and exits.*) He took my other suitcase. We better pick up a couple.

MARIO. Hold it . . . (*Finds envelope and pencil on table.*) shoot, as Bruno used to say.

GOYA. We've also got an empty room upstairs. We'll have to fill it. (MARIO *does not write, holding pencil.*) What's the matter . . . why so glum?

MARIO. Bruno was my favorite.

GOYA. Well, cheer up . . . he knows that.

MARIO. You think so?

GOYA. Hell yeah . . . Anything else the matter?

MARIO. Looks like I've got to live in this rotten old world some more. I can't seem to die.

GOYA. Wait it out . . . see who goes first.

MARIO. And I keep worrying . . . what if I live long enough to see the Republicans out of power and the Democrats come back and they're just as bad.

GOYA. Both of them are rotten and old. The way I see it Mario, everything that's bothering you is rotten and old and getting older by the minute. The solutions seem to be to outlive them . . . I mean . . . Christ . . . All you've got to do is outlive the sonsofbitches. Anything else?

MARIO. I don't think so.

GOYA. Well . . . you'll tell me if something comes up.

MARIO. Roger. You do the same.

GOYA. I'll think about it! You find out anything about the man upstairs?

MARIO. Yeah . . . your cousin says he's Irish?

GOYA. Irish . . . they make good cousins, I hear . . . HEY SEAN! HEY COUSIN! (CLIENT, *hereafter* SEAN, *appears at the top of the stairs in undershorts.*)

SEAN. My name's not Sean.

GOYA. Don't be so hasty. Try it out for a week and see what you think. Put some clothes on . . . **we've got things to do.**

SEAN. They're all wet.

GOYA. That's all right. We're not formal around here. (SEAN *disappears.* GOYA *turns to* MARIO.) I think it's time we made another trip to the orphanage, Mario.

MARIO. I think you're right.

GOYA. I bet you anything they've got some little beauties there . . .

MARIO. And I bet we're going to get one of them.

GOYA. You bet.

MARIO. What'll it be this time . . . boy or a girl?

GOYA. We'll have to put it to a vote. (SEAN *comes down the stairs.*) You're just in time to cast your ballot. GRANDPA! (OLD MAN *comes out of his room eating an apple.*)

OLD MAN. You don't have to shout . . . I'm not deaf . . . I can still hear . . . and I say we get a girl. (SEAN *goes up to the* OLD MAN.)

SEAN. Hello . . . my name's . . .

OLD MAN. I know . . . you're Sean. (GOYA *goes to the door. Opens it. Motions to others.*)

GOYA. After you . . . I love to see men parading past me . . . (*As they do.*) I know what . . . let's take Dodo with us . . . We're bound to make a good impression at the orphanage. (*They both laugh and exit as the lights fade.*)

CURTAIN

SOUND REQUIREMENTS

two 4 track stereo decks
two mixer/amplifiers
two large capacity speakers
one small capacity speaker for bathroom (must fit behind toilet)
switching arrangement to transfer s. r. speaker output to bath
DPDT Switch in box (NO CENTER OFF POSITION)
 Observe polarity
s. l. speaker located in relation to Window s. l. and front
s. r. speaker located in relation to kitchen window
 door
bath speaker as indicated
one amplifier handles Stage Left and is fed by one side of deck
 A and one side of deck B
other amplifier handles Stage Right and bath and is fed by one
 side of Deck A and one side of Deck B
(see schematic below)

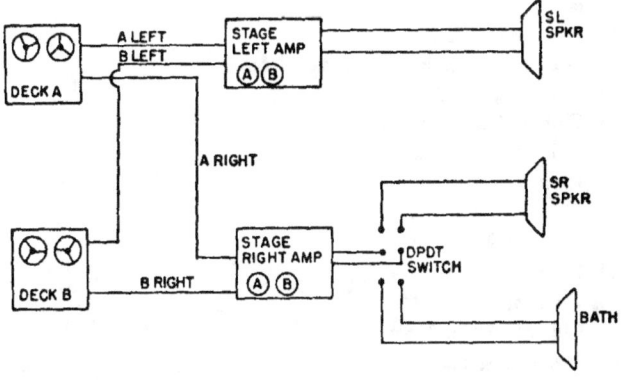

SOUND EFFECTS

1. Westminster Chimes: 9:00 AM
2. Dog howl (anguished)
3. Howl
4. Howl
5. Howl
6. Howl
7. Howl
8. Howl
9. Howl
10. Howl
11. Chimes: 4:00 PM
12. Howl
13. Dog's anguished screech
14. Two types police siren, shots, running, dog barking (montage)
15. Car starts and leaves
16. Sound of urinating in middle of bowl
17. Toilet flush
18. Chimes (12:00 midnight)
19. Chimes: 2:00 AM
20. Howl
21. Chimes: 4:00 AM
22. Chimes: 9:00 AM
23. Rain
24. Thunder
25. Chimes: 12:00 Noon
26. Happy dog bark

SET DRESSING

pile of rubbish D. S. wall of D. R. proscenium opening—boxes, newspapers, small hamper and rake
wooden box D. S. of refrigerator
dressing in refrigerator
bread box on refrigerator
toaster on bread box
napkins (paper) in holder in front of bread box
pile of dishes in sink
roll of paper towels behind sink
Ajax can behind sink
stacked regular coffee cups
orange coffee mug
extra pots on stove
magazines and papers in sideboard
ski poles D. S. of sideboard
old pair of boots on floor
pair of boots on lower railing of stairs
overcoat on hat rack
jacket with beret for Mario
knit cardigan sweater for Goya
picture over sideboard (old man and woman)
small sconce with ceramic bird over sideboard
lighting sconce (fixture) on stair wall near top
stand up (indirect light) fixture D. S. of sideboard (not practical)
baseball bat D. S. of sideboard
fuse box S. L. wall by stove
calendar beneath and U. S. of it

RUNNING PROPS AND FURNITURE

refrigerator
sink (practical with running water. Use enema bag into adapter)
stove
pan
coffee in pan (mixture of grape juice, water and food coloring)
hot mat on window sill
six demi-tasse cups and saucers on left side of stove
empty water tumbler D. S. of cups
old green hand towel left of stove
coffee can (Turkish)
spoon
ash tray
packet of matches (practical)
kitchen table with ample under leg room, lagged to floor
    Dimensions; 24" x 48"
oilcloth table cloth
magazines, and old mail
envelopes (used) to write on
at least four pencils
at least six packs of matches
package of cigarettes (Dorals)
one metal ash tray
one plastic ash tray
one sugar bowl (no sugar)
sugar spoon in bowl
three kitchen chairs
one kitchen chair D. R. wall
sideboard S. L. wall
typewriter in case U. S. end (practical)
purse (costumes, but included in prop pre-set)
half-full package of cigarettes
magazines and mail, both ends
telephone with cord at least six feet (secured)
calling card tucked under D. S. foot of telephone

RUNNING PROPS AND FURNITURE   63

In Sideboard Drawer:
   one toy gun to match real gun
   one real gun on D. S. end of drawer facing U. S.
   one telescope
   one shelf clock that looks like it might chime, D. S. end of sideboard
manual doorbell in front door
one sofa S. L. wall under window
doily on sofa
two pillows on sofa
one arm chair
one small radiator lagged securely to floor
pipe in flange U. S. of radiator to appear to go into radiator

Props II:
   coffee table (braced with pipe so it can be sat on)
   magazines on both ends of table
   small ceramic bowl to hold matches and pencil
   package of cigarettes
   hat rack U. S. of front door (dressed)

Off Stage Left:
   pair of handcuffs with trick link
   one camera in case (practical) GAF or Cannon is right
   set of keys with key for cuffs on them
   one billy club
   one police type notebook
   extra pile of old magazines
   three New York Posts folded open and in half to want ads
      one ad circled lower right of page (must be in same place)
   on top of paper 1. Magazine "Psychology Today"
   on top of paper 2. half filled bottle of German booze (water)
   near paper 3. Umbrella
   one small table near front door to help Criminal get into position
   bathroom with toilet and lavatory sink (not practical)
   fluorescent lighting (practical)

Offstage Right (GRAMPS *room*):
   small table (big enough for designated props and to type on)
   stool
   towel on table

notepaper
pencils
one apple (practical)
one paring knife

Upstairs Room:
one suitcase with shawl (costumes) through handle
one suitcase (weighted)
chair
key on nail for handcuffs (practical)

Upstairs (GOYA's *room*):
chair
ash tray
extra pencils

COSTUMES

Goya: brown slacks, tacky print pull over shirt, plain knit indoor cardigan sweater (pinkish), bathrobe, not bright floral print, heavy wool cardigan sweater, Norwegian type, simple shoes, socks, etc.

Mario: brown or dark grey work pants, print shirt (green with white dots), plaid tie, sport jacket, brown wool dressed with political button, soft hat, brown (Fedora), light brown Eisenhower jacket, dark brown beret with button on it

Sylvia: red velvet dress, very decollette, high, flashy platform shoes, heavy ribbed corduroy robe, light green and somewhat faded, dark green belt, more like bandana, beige print bandana to wear, white satin nightgown with zippered access to left breast, happy, almost hippy dress

Criminal: worn jeans, worn jeans jacket, knit shirt, pullover with horizontal colored stripes, sneakers

Bruno: police uniform complete with belt, holster, radio, accessories, slacks, sports shirt, print, brown jacket, boxer shorts, print, P.A.L. "T" shirt

Gramps: tweed pants with striped suspenders, matching vest or cardigan sweater, long john top, red baseball cap, boxer shorts, overcoat (dressing on hat rack)

Studley: full police uniform with billy club

Adolph: suit, overcoat, tan, hat, tie, shoes

Client: jacket, pants (not matching), vest, boxer shorts, T shirt, very long ugly tie, shoes, shirt

SCENE DESIGN
"NOURISH THE BEAST"

Note: There is a platform above bath for Goya's room.

MUSIC USE NOTE

Licensees are solely responsible for obtaining formal written permission from copyright owners to use copyrighted music in the performance of this play and are strongly cautioned to do so. If no such permission is obtained by the licensee, then the licensee must use only original music that the licensee owns and controls. Licensees are solely responsible and liable for all music clearances and shall indemnify the copyright owners of the play(s) and their licensing agent, Samuel French, against any costs, expenses, losses and liabilities arising from the use of music by licensees. Please contact the appropriate music licensing authority in your territory for the rights to any incidental music.

IMPORTANT BILLING AND CREDIT REQUIREMENTS

If you have obtained performance rights to this title, please refer to your licensing agreement for important billing and credit requirements.

www.ingramcontent.com/pod-product-compliance
Lightning Source LLC
Chambersburg PA
CBHW072021290426
44109CB00018B/2305